Adventures on Turtle Island

Story by Pamela Rushby

Illustrations by Millie Liu

Adventures on Turtle Island

Text: Pamela Rushby
Publishers: Tania Mazzeo and Eliza Webb
Series consultant: Amanda Sutera
  Hands on Heads Consulting
Editor: Gemma Smith
Project editor: Annabel Smith
Designer: Jess Kelly
Project designer: Danielle Maccarone
Illustrations: Millie Liu
Production controller: Renee Tome

NovaStar

ISBN 978 0 17 033398 6

Cengage Learning Australia
Level 5, 80 Dorcas Street
Southbank VIC 3006 Australia
Phone: 1300 790 853
Email: aust.nelsonprimary@cengage.com

For learning solutions, visit **cengage.com.au**

Printed in China by 1010 Printing International Ltd
1 2 3 4 5 6 7 28 27 26 25 24

Nelson acknowledges the Traditional Owners and Custodians of the lands of all First Nations Peoples. We pay respect to Elders past and present, and extend that respect to all First Nations Peoples today.

Contents

Chapter 1   Exploring the Islands   5

Chapter 2   Ashore   9

Chapter 3   A Stranded Turtle   15

Chapter 4   Uncle Lucas!   23

Chapter 1

Exploring the Islands

Lucas leaned over the side of the boat and kept a lookout for turtles. Uncle Ollie had told him they'd see thousands!

Lucas and his uncle were having a holiday on Uncle Ollie's boat. They were staying on board and exploring some islands in the bay. Uncle Ollie knew the area well.

Today was going to be special. They had planned on visiting a small island where the turtles came to lay their eggs every nesting season.

"We won't go ashore though," said Uncle Ollie. "Turtle Island is a protected turtle rookery, and these turtles are an endangered species. But I'm sure we'll see lots of female turtles swimming towards the island."

Suddenly, a round head popped out of the clear water.

"There!" Lucas shouted. "A turtle. And another. They're everywhere!"

Soon, the small island appeared. Lucas stared at it.

"That's funny," he said to Uncle Ollie. "You said the island is protected. But there's a boat there. And there are people on the island, too."

Chapter 2

Ashore

Uncle Ollie peered through his binoculars. Then he smiled. "It's all right," he said. "The people are wearing National Park uniforms. They're allowed to be there. But I'll radio their boat and ask if everything is okay."

Archie, the head ranger, knew Uncle Ollie.

"We're fine, Ollie," Archie radioed back.
"But maybe you'd like to come ashore
and see what we're doing?"

Soon, Lucas and Uncle Ollie dropped anchor and waded to the shore.

"They're building fences," said Lucas. "But why? No one lives on this island."

Archie explained, "It's very sad. This island has many small cliffs. The turtles come ashore at night to lay their eggs. When they do, some of the turtles fall off the edges of the cliffs. If they land on their backs, they can't roll over again.
Then they'll probably die. But these fences will keep them away from the dangerous areas."

"They *die*? That's awful!" Lucas was horrified.

Another ranger, Iris, smiled at Lucas. "Until the fences are finished, we try to help the turtles. We check the beaches each morning for stranded turtles. If we find one, we turn it over and get it back into the water. It's hard work. They can weigh up to a hundred kilograms. Maybe you and your uncle could stay for a few days and help us build the fences?"

"Could we?" Lucas asked.

"Why not?" said Uncle Ollie. "We can help on the island during the day and sleep on the boat at night."

Chapter 3

A Stranded Turtle

Everyone worked hard on the fences over the next few days. It was hot, and they all grew tired, but each morning there were fewer stranded turtles than the day before. Everyone was delighted. But there was more work to do.

The rangers had started tagging the turtles.

"We'd really like to know if the turtles return to the island to lay more than once a season," Iris told Lucas and Uncle Ollie. "You see, turtles lay about a hundred eggs at a time. Then they swim back out to sea."

Iris continued, "We think they might return and lay another batch of eggs, up to ten times a season. So, we're painting a stripe on their shells, once they've laid. If we see a turtle with a stripe, we know it's been here before."

"You could help, Lucas," said Archie.
"Could you walk right around the island
and check for tagged turtles? It's a small
island, so it'll only take about half an hour."

"Sure!" said Lucas, and he set off.

On the far side of the island, Lucas saw
something moving on the beach. He ran
up to it. It was an overturned turtle. He
tried to roll it over, but it was too heavy.

Lucas quickly ran back to Uncle Ollie and the rangers.

"There's a stranded turtle!" Lucas shouted.

Uncle Ollie, Archie and Iris followed Lucas back to the turtle.

"It looks like she'd laid her eggs and was heading for the sea," said Archie.

"Let's get her on her way," said Iris. "Ready, everyone? Heave!"

The turtle didn't move.

"Again," said Archie, puffing. "One, two, three!"

This time, the turtle rolled over.

"Well done!" Iris said. "Now we need to paint a stripe on her."

"Can I paint an 'L' for Lucas?" asked Lucas.

"Sure," Iris laughed.

They all watched as the turtle swam away.

Chapter 4

Uncle Lucas!

A few days later, just as it was getting dark, Lucas, Uncle Ollie and the rangers walked along the beach. They were watching for turtles coming ashore.

"Look!" shouted Lucas suddenly. "It's my turtle! She's come back to lay more eggs."

"How do you feel about becoming 'Uncle Lucas' to hundreds of baby turtles?" asked Archie, smiling.

"Great!" laughed Lucas. "As long as I don't have to buy them all birthday presents!"